DIGITAL CITIZENSHIP

FINDING INFORMATION

by Kristine Spanier, MLIS

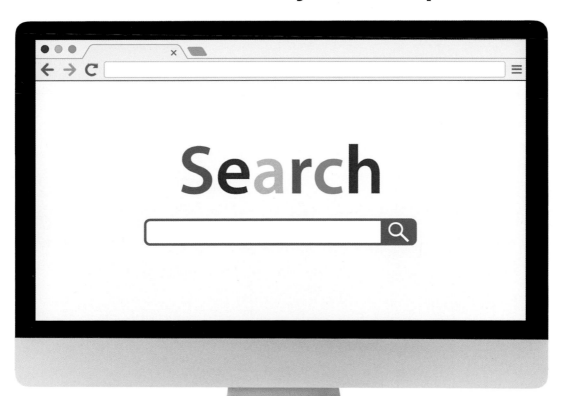

Ideas for Parents and Teachers

Pogo Books let children practice reading informational text while introducing them to nonfiction features such as headings, labels, sidebars, maps, and diagrams, as well as a table of contents, glossary, and index.

Carefully leveled text with a strong photo match offers early fluent readers the support they need to succeed.

Before Reading

- "Walk" through the book and point out the various nonfiction features. Ask the student what purpose each feature serves.
- Look at the glossary together. Read and discuss the words.

Read the Book

- Have the child read the book independently.
- Invite him or her to list questions that arise from reading.

After Reading

- Discuss the child's questions. Talk about how he or she might find answers to those questions.
- Prompt the child to think more. Ask: What did you know about different sources of information before you read this book?

Pogo Books are published by Jump!
5357 Penn Avenue South
Minneapolis, MN 55419
www.jumplibrary.com

Library of Congress Cataloging-in-Publication Data

Names: Spanier, Kristine, author.
Title: Finding information / by Kristine Spanier, MLIS.
Description: Minneapolis, MN: Jump!, [2019]
Series: Digital citizenship | Includes index.
Identifiers: LCCN 2018035312 (print)
LCCN 2018041696 (ebook)
ISBN 9781641284431 (ebook)
ISBN 9781641284417 (hardcover: alk. paper)
ISBN 9781641284424 (pbk.)
Subjects: LCSH: Research—Methodology—Juvenile literature. | Information resources—Juvenile literature.
Classification: LCC ZA3080 (ebook) | LCC ZA3080 .S66 2019 (print) | DDC 028.7—dc23
LC record available at https://lccn.loc.gov/2018035312

Editor: Jenna Trnka
Designer: Michelle Sonnek

Photo Credits: Africa Studio/Shutterstock, cover (books); Aiolos Design/Shutterstock, cover (tablet); Naruedom Yaempongsa/Shutterstock, 1 (computer); Hi-Vector/Shutterstock, 1 (screen); Coprid/Shutterstock, 3; Valentina_G/Shutterstock, 4 (chocolate); Simone van den Berg/Shutterstock, 4 (dog); mirtmirt/Shutterstock, 5 (background); Apic/RETIRED/Getty, 5 (screen left); Ipsumpix/Getty, 5 (screen right); Pictorial Press Ltd/Alamy, 6-7 (foreground); Bliss Hunter Images/Shutterstock, 6-7 (background); prapann/Shutterstock, 8 (notebook); BonD80/Shutterstock, 8 (pen); Davizro Photography/Shutterstock, 9; GUNDAM_Ai/Shutterstock, 10-11; Sergey Novikov/Shutterstock, 12-13; Marek Walica/Shutterstock, 14-15; Apollofoto/Shutterstock, 16; Alex Veresovich/Shutterstock, 17; JPC-PROD/Shutterstock, 18-19; David Franklin/Shutterstock, 20-21; monticello/Shutterstock, 23 (books and tablet); Rawpixel.com/Shutterstock, 23 (screen).

Printed in the United States of America at Corporate Graphics in North Mankato, Minnesota.

TABLE OF CONTENTS

CHAPTER 1

ASK QUESTIONS

Should dogs eat chocolate? Who flew the first airplane? We ask questions every day. We want answers.

These **facts** can be found using a **search engine**. An example is Google. It searches thousands of websites. It tells us chocolate is dangerous for dogs. What else? That the Wright Brothers flew the first airplane.

The Wright Brothers' First Flight

website

Some questions are harder to answer. Like what? Let's say you have to write a report. Your **topic** is the American Revolution (1775–1783). You have to write about the events that led to it. Researching this takes more time. Why? There are many **sources** on this topic. There is more than one answer. Where do you start?

DID YOU KNOW?

In the past, most information was printed. In books. Magazines. Newspapers. Now we can access **digital** information.

NEWS

CHAPTER 2

CHOOSE SOURCES

First, make sure you have a clear topic. Write down your question. Is it too simple? Dig deeper. Is it too broad? Simplify it. Underline the **keywords**. These are the most important words. They define your topic.

What are the <u>events</u> that <u>led</u> to the <u>American Revolution</u>?

keywords

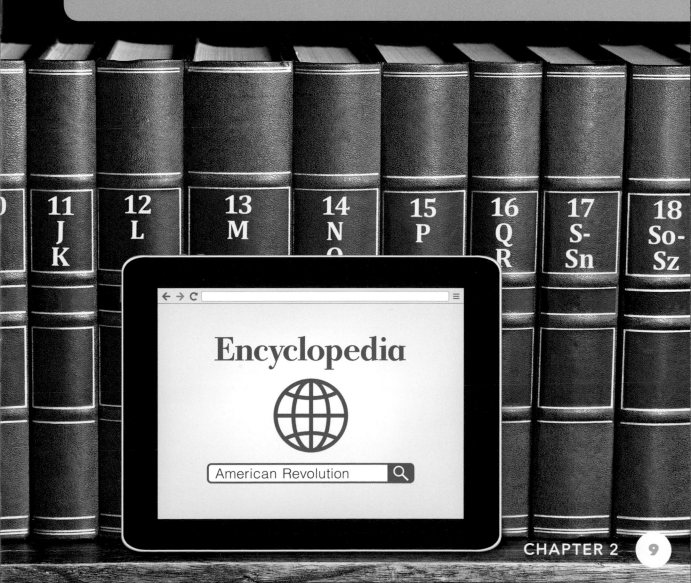

Start with an encyclopedia. You can find one online. Or in a library. Search "American Revolution." You'll get information about battles. Important people. This information will help you. It can give you ideas about what else to look for.

Library **catalogs** list books and other sources you can use. They also provide **databases**. You may need a library card to use them.

Librarians know where to find information. They can help! Tell them your question. And what you have found so far. Ask them where else you should look.

TAKE A LOOK!

Here are some popular sources. What are the differences between them?

index – Shows where to find topics in a book. Topics are in an alphabetical list.

magazine – Includes articles and photos. Can be published monthly or weekly.

newspaper – Includes articles, letters, and photos. Can be printed or digital.

reference book – Includes easy-to-find information. Examples are encyclopedias and atlases.

website – Made up of digital files. The most trusted information can be found on .edu or .org sites.

Search different sources using your keywords. Create a list of those with the best information. Make sure your information is **reliable**. And current. If it is from a long time ago, the information may be outdated.

Now read your sources. Take notes. Make sure to write down the sources. You will need to list them. You may find a phrase that you want to include. Put quotation marks around it. We do this to give credit to the source.

WHAT DO YOU THINK?

Don't copy sources word-for-word. This is **plagiarism**. Does your school have rules against it? Why is this important?

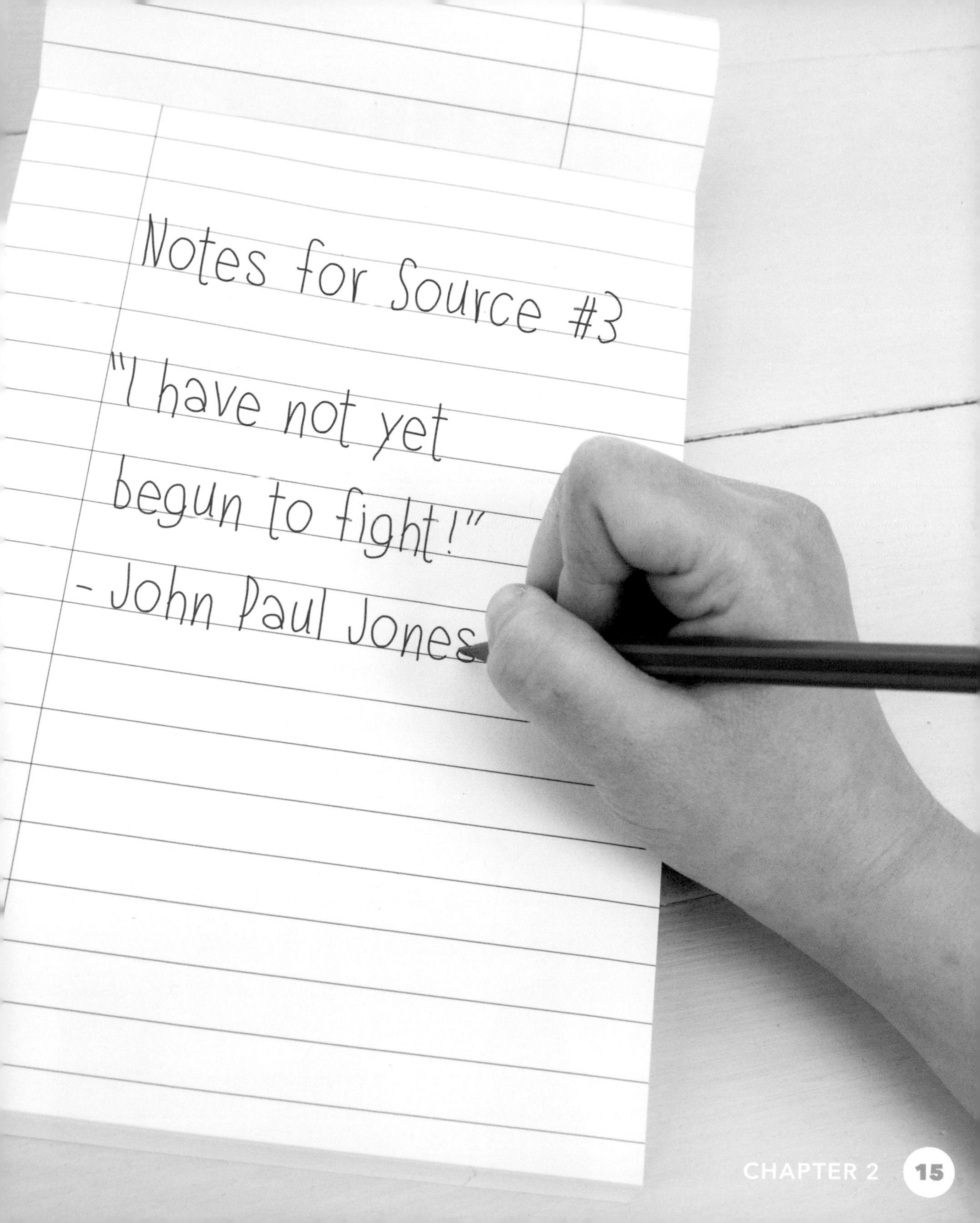
Notes for Source #3
"I have not yet
begun to fight!"
- John Paul Jones

CHAPTER 3

ORGANIZE AND PRESENT

You have found your sources. You have taken notes. Now it is time to organize your information.

Work at a big table or
on the floor. What are the
key ideas? Sort your notes
so that they fit into one
of these topics. This will
help you write your report.

You're ready to write! Start with a sentence that introduces your main topic. Write two more that support it. Begin a new paragraph. Use your notes to help you tell your story. Your last paragraph should **summarize** your report. Make sure to end with a great closing sentence!

Create a list of the books you used. Include page numbers and authors. List databases and websites, too. This is your **citations list.**

Finding good information is an important skill. You can learn about any topic that interests you!

WHAT DO YOU THINK?

How did finding sources go? What worked? What did not work? What would you do differently next time?

author

title

Citations List

Doe, Jane. The American Revolution. Minneapolis, MN: Good Book Company, 2018. Print.

publisher

publication date

"Ten Facts about Washington and the ~~ry War." George Washington's ~~rnon, 2018, https://www. mountvernon.org/george-washington/ the-revolutionary-war/ten-facts-about- the-revolutionary-war/. Accessed 18 Oct. 2018. Web.

ACTIVITIES & TOOLS

TAKE ACTION!

FINDING THE BEST SOURCES

How do you decide which sources are best? Filter them using this set of questions.

❶ Do you understand the information? It should be written for your reading level.

❷ Is it relevant to your research? It should answer some of your questions.

❸ Is the copyright date current? This is the year it was published.

❹ Does the author have knowledge of the subject? He or she should be an expert in your topic.

❺ Who published the information? The publisher should have a reputation for producing quality information.

❻ Is the information accurate? Try finding it in a second place. This is called fact-checking.

GLOSSARY

catalogs: Searchable lists of sources in libraries.

citations list: A list of sources cited and used.

databases: Large collections of information that are organized and stored in computers for quick searching.

digital: Electronic and computerized.

facts: Pieces of information that are known to be true.

keywords: Words that can be used to find a particular book, website, or computer file.

plagiarism: Stealing the ideas or words of another and presenting them as your own.

reliable: Able to be trusted.

search engine: A computer program used to search data for specific information.

sources: Books or other documents that provide information.

summarize: To give a brief statement that gives the main points or ideas of something.

topic: The subject of a discussion, speech, lesson, study, or piece of writing.

INDEX

TO LEARN MORE

Finding more information is as easy as 1, 2, 3.

1 Go to www.factsurfer.com

2 Enter "findinginformation" into the search box.

3 Click the "Surf" button to see a list of websites.

FACT SURFER